Poūkahangatus

Poūkahangatus

Tayi Tibble

ALFRED A. KNOPF

New York   2022

THIS IS A BORZOI BOOK
PUBLISHED BY ALFRED A. KNOPF

Copyright © 2018 by Tayi Tibble

All rights reserved. Published in the United States by Alfred A. Knopf,
a division of Penguin Random House LLC, New York, and distributed in
Canada by Penguin Random House Canada Limited, Toronto. Originally
published in New Zealand by Victoria University of Wellington Press,
Wellington, in 2018.

www.aaknopf.com

Knopf, Borzoi Books, and the colophon are registered trademarks of
Penguin Random House LLC.

Portions of this work originally appeared in the following publications:
Turbine: "Poūkahangatus: An Essay About Indigenous Hair Dos and
Don'ts" (2017); *The Spinoff:* "In the 1960s an Influx of Māori Women"
(December 15, 2017), "Ode to Johnsonville's Cindy Crawford"
(July 13, 2018), and "Assimilation" (August 21, 2018); *Poetry Magazine:*
"Identity Politics" (February 2018).

Library of Congress Cataloging-in-Publication Data
Names: Tibble, Tayi, [date] author.
Title: Poūkahangatus / Tayi Tibble.
Description: First American edition. | New York : Alfred A. Knopf, 2022.
Identifiers: LCCN 2021043325 (print) | LCCN 2021043326 (ebook) |
ISBN 9780593534601 (hardcover) | ISBN 9780593534618 (ebook)
Subjects: LCGFT: Poetry.
Classification: LCC PR9639.4.T45 P68 2022 (print) |
LCC PR9639.4.T45 ebook) | DDC 821/.92—dc23
LC record available at https://lccn.loc.gov/2021043325
LC ebook record available at https://lccn.loc.gov/2021043326

Jacket art by Simone Noronha
Jacket design by Linda Huang

Illustrations by dimensi_design/Shutterstock.com

Manufactured in Canada
First American Edition

For Mum

CONTENTS

3

Poūkahangatus

Poūkahangatus

AN ESSAY ABOUT INDIGENOUS HAIR DOS AND DON'TS

In the Beginning

The earliest memory to survive the red fog of infancy reveals your great-grandmother on her bed, cutting the thick peppery plait falling down her back with a blunt pair of orange-handled scissors. Remember the resistance. Imagine if the ropes of Māui had snapped and the world had been plunged back into the womb of darkness. After she died, you found it again, coiled and paled like the skin of an ancient snake. You held it to your throat, between her unwanted fur coats, and felt like Cleopatra deciding not to wait for the Romans.

How Not to Be Dead in a Year of Snakes

According to Greek mythology, according to Wikipedia, Medusa was a 'monster'; she is generally described as a winged human female with venomous snakes in place of hair. Gazers upon her 'hideous' face would turn to stone. However, it is less known that Medusa was a master carver, engraving her existence in bone forever. Anything else said about her is a rumour and a violent appropriation. In fact, it must be difficult not to sprout a head of snakes in a society that constantly hisses at you.

Samson and Delilah

When I was thirteen I secretly straightened my hair with my nana's iron in an attic. From then on, I crushed myself skinny between hot metal plates every morning. The smell of dead ends burning was the scent of prayer candles. *Ake Ake Ake, Amene.*

Starry Nights in Nelson

My nana is a wallflower, but a flower nonetheless. This means she
is always being looked at and looked at—at her expense. When
she was born, she was born with a new kind of beauty. The type
that truly ached in the fifties. Brown skin stretched over white
stock bones. She had her father's height and his perfect featureless
features set alight by the warmth of her mother's black sand eyes
and hair, but hers was so long and so straight that it was dizzying
to look at—like looking at the stars in a place where there is only
sky and feeling awed but terrified by the great burning darkness.
It's the kind of beauty that makes men crash cars, abandon wives
and launch ships. Unfortunately for her, all this is very loud and
my nana is a wallflower, but a flower nonetheless.

The Waikato Wars

When I lie in the bath, I fill up the tub with blue-black hair, bruised
and swampy. I imagine that I am a nineteenth-century body of a
mother in the Waikato, forced from my pā, fleeing in the forest.
I am found swollen in a watery grave.

A Step-by-Step Guide to Dying

Relax. Wash hair with tears. Condition with Kumarika oil, coconut
oil, olive oil of the ancient Greek kind. Relax. Egg whites for a
hot glossy shine. Gasoline for hot glossy shine. Light a match
for an edgy new cut. Distressed is in. Relax. Buy a box of Nordic
blond every full moon but never use it. This is imperative. Rinse
thoroughly with intergenerational trauma and pink water. Blow-dry
straight with a 1950s gold soft-paddle brush made from the hair of
the finest palomino ponies. Now take a step back and relax. Admire
your silky manageable mane.

Poūkahangatus

In 1995 I was born and Walt Disney's Animated Classic *Pocahontas* was released. Have you ever heard a wolf cry to the blue corn moon? Mum has. I howled when my mother told me Pocahontas was real but went with John Smith to England and got a disease and died. Representation is important.

The Pussycat Dolls

Nicole Scherzinger was born in Honolulu, Hawai'i. Nicole Scherzinger was born into a Catholic family. Nicole Scherzinger's parents separated when she was just a baby. Nicole Scherzinger moved with her mother to Louisville, Kentucky. Nicole Scherzinger admits that while growing up, her family did not have a lot of money. Nicole Scherzinger thanks her mother for all the support she gave her to become what she is today. Nicole Scherzinger was the only Pacific Island Princess I ever saw in the centre of a TV screen, so in maths class we practise swinging our chairs out from behind us while grinding our hips and untying our hair. We loosen the buttons of our school shirts, accordingly. I dead-eye the teacher. Don't you wish your girlfriend was hot like me and Nicole Scherzinger?

Starless Nights in Wellington

In a hotel room, a man runs his hands through your hair like a surveyor. He is surprised when he asks you if it's dyed. Groans when he tells you that he has never seen hair that black before. But what he really means is skin, what he really means is you've been a bad bad girl, what he really means is I don't typically fuck with minority races but I still want to fuck you. He touches you in a place that makes you wish your hair was a crown of snakes, but it's not enough to make you leave. Your mouth is a perpetual O that looks like a yes please and never a no. Representation is important.

Science and Religion

Hair colour is the pigmentation of follicles due to two types of melanin: eumelanin and pheomelanin. If more eumelanin is present, the hair is darker; if less eumelanin is present, the hair is lighter. The darker a person's natural hair colour, the more individual hair follicles they have on their scalp. When a person's natural hair colour is darker, the eyes tend to match. If the eyes are the window to the soul, then we are soulless, plunged back into darkness and floating between worlds.

Politics and Activism

I have decided to tactically develop a crush on Hone Harawira. This is for my sanity and protection. In order to achieve this I am rebranding as a Black Panther. Turtle necks, aviators and Ranginui Walker. Ka Whawhai Tonu Mātou are the only Māori words I know. I know it's not enough. But damn it's a good few words to start with!

We Will Fight!

Everyone talks about my 17-year-old sister's hair to the point that it causes her anxiety. She wants to get a trim, but she has to negotiate her colonial guilt with our ancestors first. Personally, as the eldest, I inherit the most mana. I will do us both a favour and cut it while she is sleeping.

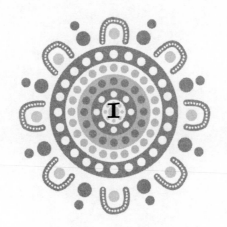

I

In the 1960s an Influx of Māori Women

Move to Tinakori Road in their printed mini dresses.
Grow flowers on white stone rooftops to put
in their honeycomb vases. Dust the pussy-shaped
ashtray their husbands bought on vacation in Sydney.
Walk to Kirkcaldie and Stains while their husbands are at work.
Spend their monthly allowance on a mint-green margarita mixer.
Buy makeup at Elizabeth Arden in the shade too-pale-pink.
Buy vodka and dirty magazines on the way home from the chemist.
Hide the vodka and dirty magazines in the spare refrigerator
in the basement. Telephone their favourite sister in Gisborne.
Go out to dinner with their husbands and dance with his friends.
Smile at the wives who refuse to kiss their ghost-pink cheeks.
Order desserts like pecan pie but never eat it. Eat two pieces
of white bread in the kitchen with the light off. Slip into an apricot
nylon nightgown freshly ordered off a catalogue. Keep quiet
with their husbands' blue-veined arms corseting their waists.
Remember the appointment they made to get their hair fixed on
Lambton Quay. Think about drowning themselves in the bathtub
instead. Resurface with clean skin, then rinse and repeat.

I Wear Aviators to the Club

It took me about six months of entertaining the idea but now I wear them every weekend. They help me keep my chin up when heads are hitting the table. It's like an episode of the old *Charlie's Angels* except Charlie is a drag queen named Harlie Lux and luxe lycra jumpsuits are coming back into fashion. I used to have a David Bowie sticker on my laptop. But after he died it was like a tiny ghost of a genderless angel lit up by green charger light. And it was so sad. No longer a gang patch for melodramatic writer girls and gay boys in tight pants but a thorn on one side of my keyboard, and kind of morbid, like when Samoans wear T-shirts emblazoned with warped images of their dead relatives. I had to scrape it off, and it was like picking a friend up off the sidewalk and watching them disintegrate in your arms. Every relationship leaves behind a sticky residue, hard to wash away without chemical help. I prefer liquor and looks so strong that they make my eyes water. But whatever keeps the party lit and the lushes from gushing on the dancefloor.

The Warehouse

Obviously I am Edie Sedgwick
in last night's eyelashes slept in and cried on.

You are always skinnier after a weekend-long bender.
Obviously you are Andy Warhol but—*gayer*, somehow.

Everything you wear shares the consistency
of a second skin which is a snake-like impulse but—

if you are a snake then I am a snake
charmer making you dance in the Warehouse, hungover.

In the lingerie aisle, I pose for your camera
like a muse in 15-denier stockings, shredding.

We sample the candles critically like they are
perfumes and we are hunters looking for—

base notes of Campbell's soup or anything strong enough
to cover up the scent of spewed hearts in the apartment

carpet the release of last night's ego, and don't forget
to put the brillo in the basket before we go.

Our Nan Lets Us Smoke Inside

but only when we drink wine and play cards
on the kitchen table. I feel glamorous
when I drop my ash into the pāua shell in the middle.

Our nan wears black leather pumps
and dries wishbones from chicken carcasses
in an empty margarine container on top of the fridge.

She's not my real nan
but I have always wished she was.
I wished I was born with her

blood in my veins, her dark
Waikato DNA, high cheekbones
and heavy wet eyes just like my sister.

Our nan met her late husband
in the late sixties. She was dressed
in a little mod dress, her black hair flipped.

He was a cowboy with mutton chops and tan-lined legs
in short cream shorts, who rode off to work
every morning with a commercial digger for a horse but—

he'd pick us up in his station wagon on Sundays.
Johnny Cash and his metronome voice making us
fall asleep against the dusty windows so we would stop

for a Filet-O-Fish and a strawberry milkshake
for lunch and dinner, but he always picked
my sister up more.

At his funeral,
us girls carried the mismatched flowers
behind our brothers in black sunglasses.

At the service,
we all got up and sang *I hope you're dancing in the sky*
but it was painful and flat and sounded like coughing.

During the burial,
nobody exhaled a word as my nan ashed out
a half-sucked cigarette in the fresh sour soil.

In the car park,
we all smoked back tears with another cigarette pacifier
like babies numbed on a nicotine nipple.

Tangi in the King Country

The Grass.

The first time the children were driven deep into the King Country, the sky was overcast and never cleared. After eight hours in the car they swung the door out and gasped, their little lungs drunk on stale air. They collapsed onto the grass which after the stiff tan leather of station-wagon seats was soft and meaty. They lay on their backs and tried to relax their muscles, which were tired from fighting for dominion over the middle-seat armrest. But they were told off by a stranger, who told them to call her Aunty in a stern kind of way that they were unused to hearing and nearly made them cry. When she finally dropped her opal, pūkana eyes, she stared towards the soil. *The grass is sacred, it is still watered by old blood.* That was enough. They didn't ask again but they were desperate to know, whose blood?

The Smell.

There are no morgues that deep in the King Country; instead the body is treated with animal fats and salts and washed in the river. But by the third day, the smell of grease and a hundred thrashing bodies sleeping began to stain and stick to everything. At first they were bemused at how the smell got everywhere, how it seemed to sit in the skull, in the sinuses, on the back of the teeth and on the upturn of their nanny's lips especially. But then it became sickening and thick, as if it would kill them, like gas left on. At night they took to burying themselves down the other end of their sleeping bags, where it was dark and tight and more than one of them got claustrophobic. Hera, the eldest but not by much, had thought to pick flowers from the back by the hāngi pit and they took turns holding them to their noses as if they were sleep-inducing opiates but they were bitter and soggy and smelt like dirt and wet foliage, but it was a gesture, and better than the dark rot that seemed to stick to everything, and later, as they would discover, even clung to memory.

The Food.

They reckoned all the food was soft because all the old nannies had gummy smiles. The cabbage was boiled to the point of liquid. The white bread, damp and smothered in margarine. The nannies disgustingly dipped it into little brown cups of cuppa-tea. The pork and chicken fell apart at the lightest touch and were popular with everyone, the small children especially. The 'other meats' were suspicious and wild. They avoided the crunchy tiny birds and gelatinous globs of cold grey eel which Hera touched, squealing. One of their new cousins showed them how to use fry bread like a sponge, mopping up spilled sugar from the plastic tablecloths and then eating it. The blobs of half-cooked dough served in a soup of weeds and dirty roots was the worst, but the most fun. Hemi, the youngest but not by much, tucked a lump into his pocket. He wanted to take one home to show to his friends or his teacher. On second thoughts he snatched another, to later throw at his sister.

The Burial.

They had a cry because everyone else was having a cry. Hera encouraged Hemi to have a crack at making the long kind of whale noises the nannies made, which was swiftly met with a hard kick in the arse from their father. Confused by this, Hemi went on to prod all the crying nannies in the bum, which made his mum oscillate between shame and shameful stifled laughter. So he was grabbed and made to hold hands with his dad at the back, and he was mad because Tama laughed at him and gave him the fingers, but mostly he was mad because he could no longer see the earth, waiting to swallow the coffin in a single hungry bite.

The Ghosts.

They washed their hands because everyone else was washing their
hands. There were two sawn-off milk bottles and a mossy trough
filled with rainwater. They watched their mother make the shape
of a cross across her chest while the nannies tossed handfuls over
their shoulders, so they copied but with tactful aim, again and again,
until their father got so mad that they were sent to bed with no tea
and no Chocolate Thins for supper. Angry in their sleeping bags,
Hera told them that she had heard from their mean aunty that if
they didn't wash their hands seriously then the ghosts would come
and pull their eyeballs out, which made Hemi too scared to close his
eyes, and in the middle of the night he woke Hera up with desperate
puppy begging. He asked her soft and whakamā to please take him
to the bathroom and help him wash his hands again, just to be sure.

The Goodbye.

Hemi made it through the night, and in the morning Dad said they were going home but before they could leave they had to clean. They helped stack all the mattresses in the middle and had to resist bouncing on the pile like a trampoline because the mean aunty was watching them with beady eyes that followed them everywhere like the wooden men on the walls. Hemi wondered if the men hadn't washed their hands right either and that's why their pupils were made of pāua. Hemi cried for the next hour and hid under the car. After the final karakia, Mum, Dad and Hera came and found him. *Go give your aunty a kiss!* She had sloppy juju lips that blubbered all over him as she kissed him and called him *Bubba*. Hera laughed and Dad looked stressed. Mum said she was sad to go.

Agenda

Rise from the dead.
Speak to the devil.
Coordinate hand games
to the books of the Bible.
Complete an A4 dot-to-dot
of Lot's wife turning into salt.
Thank Jehovah for the salt
bread, rice, beans and chicken
we are about to receive.
Let the dog receive them instead.
Get off the fucking table
and go to bed.

Sensitivity

248 years
since Captain Cook
landed

14 years
since *Whale Rider* was
released

Keisha Castle-Hughes
is speared through the heart
by a white man with a ship

in the television series
Game of Thrones
season 7 episode 3
52 minutes and 22 seconds in.

Cowboys and Indians

a stone thrown by a slingshot
puckers the russet of a tiny cheekbone

it's the seventies and the kids play
while the mothers drink margaritas
on the orange brick patio

Susan loves the sun
since returning from
a summer Samaritan
trip to India

and she says
*Isn't it good to see the children
mixing so well?* and she seems

confident and proud

like that time that teacher
telephoned her
and said *Michael has hit a girl*

and she paused thoughtfully

for a moment
before exhaling
down the receiver

No, I think not
that doesn't quite sound like him

Mint-Green Cross

The reality is you've got a good 30 centimetres of runway where
the piles of bric-a-brac shit have been shovelled to either side with
no logic, no customer-friendly flow, no thoughtfully considered
floor plan to direct foot traffic, so if some other fucker happens to
be in there at the same time you can guarantee that at some point
you will find yourself face to face, eyes locked, hearts syncopating,
roses blooming in the cheeks. You could try, if you'd like, to step
around them, but you do so at your own risk. The dangerous
climate increases the chances of toppling into old *Vogues*, ugly 80s
handbags and broken discmans and, sure enough, what with all that
staring and blushing you have been doing, you will end up falling
in love. R has got no time for love. He is a Leo. He believes he is a
reincarnated dandy, who in turn was the reincarnation of a Roman
emperor. People part to let him through and that's why I like him,
just like the Israelites liked Moses, for the most part—at least they
did when the sea was parting; it's just impressive. Last time he was
looking for Minnie Riperton on vinyl. The time before that, a kilt
like Kurt Cobain's. The time before that time, a neon light-up sign
of Jesus. Only one of which was successfully secured. This time we
look for pulp fictions, or anything Naomi Campbell. I find a mint-
green cross in a bunch of Girl Guide badges, which I could mistake
for an omen, but R says he will make it into an earring and this
soothes me. We ask David White for the price. For no good reason
he tells us there was a matching pink cross in a little white-gold
plastic box in here just the other day, which is a shame. And anyway,
what kind of connoisseur splits up a set? Maybe he was too anxious
to protest in the name of the antique? Maybe he couldn't speak with
the walls of *National Geographics* and ceramic cats closing in around
him? Sometimes we say we hate David White, what with him being
an inconsiderate hoarder and all. The only decent thing I ever got

here was a white bell-sleeved dress that didn't fit. Sometimes I want to scream at him, you can't just call your problems something beautiful like a gallery, David.

Ode to Johnsonville's Cindy Crawford

1. Once at a Jehovah's Witness convention an old frightened man pleaded, *Adrienne? Is that you?* His face was a screwed-up ball of God-fearing agony and, accused, I blurted, *No! I'm just her daughter!* I remember the relief in his features; it was the expression of a man with his belief in religion restored, and it was absurd, watching him apprehend himself for believing, for one godless second, that the image of a child he knew once had appeared to him like the burning bush or the final sign before Armageddon.

2. During a fight you offended me when you said, *You look just like your father when you roll your eyes,* to which I replied, *I don't even know what he looks like,* which was a) excellent and well-timed and b) punctuated by a triumphant slam of my bedroom door. Behind it I spent the night looking in the mirror, trying to imagine you both in the hope that what you saw in each other might be seen in me.

3. As soon as you stepped off the ferry, boys who also had tickets for the green bus were trying to make passes and catcalling you at the dairy. Got the nickname Johnsonville's Cindy Crawford a) because of the huge mole under your nose and b) because at 17 you were going to be a proper model, but you became a proper mother instead. That said, it does bring me a motherly joy to think about which boy must have tried that line on you once. Was it at a party? Did you laugh and take it lightly? Did you file it away, a funny phrase to tell your daughter one day, when you needed to remind her that you had a life before her and that life still has a legend?

4. You were an astronaut in cyberspace. Very Y2K. Always hooked up and logged on. Had a see-through Mac and custom ringtones. Had cool friends with beepers, flat tops

and skateboards. They'd come over and play PlayStation. I'd hang out with them, on your lap like a teenager, playing *Tomb Raider* because even in unflattering PS1 pixels Lara Croft was so pretty with her long hair and big triangular boobs. Flipping through a magazine you persuaded me that a particular photo of Angelina Jolie was you. You were convincing. So was the photo. I took it to school.

5. You looked like Aaliyah. Always had the exact same haircut. Cried and played 'I Miss You' on repeat after her plane crashed in the tropics. Said a eulogy in which you told a story about doing a hula at school to one of her songs—I forget which one—because the story only becomes memorable at the part where your purple sarong starts slipping off your hips and at first you are mortified but then you just improvise and start tying the strings of your sarong back together, and via some unknown magic the specific feminine placement of your hands has a hypnotic effect that ensares the audience, like a Venus flytrap. This must have been not long before you became pregnant, although I am just paraphrasing here.

6. I had an awkward stint as a teenage witch. So sensitive folk bands fronted by depressed songstresses with bowl cuts, in an open rebellion against hip-hop. Your favourite song had lines like *Don't hate me cos I'm beautiful* and *Jealousy is the ugliest trait (don't ever do it!)* but I used to do it. I used to sit in my room and scream as it played for the 2000th time, but I knew it wouldn't take a long hard look in the mirror to figure out why I never sang along in the kitchen while you cooked.

7. *The Ugly Duckling. The Hungry Caterpillar.* Grew up reading neither. Grew up reading *Fashion Quarterly* and the Bible. After another metamorphosis you wanted to be 'more involved' and, as a result of your commitment to your children's education, schoolboys would try to text you or

add you on Facebook. The messages I received were variations of *What's your mums number?* Or, worse, *Who's your daddy?*

8. I got a man off the internet to buy me a pink velvet Juicy Couture tracksuit for a lol but you didn't realise it was a gay joke so you said I looked *glamorous but practical* and I laughed because you sounded so genuine and of course you were, because I was dressed just like you when you would go out to the clubs and drop it like it was a hot summer circa 2002.

9. Last night I texted Aniqueja, *Annoying your sister and making your mum laugh are on the same level in terms of intimacy and emotional fulfilment.* She replied, *Oi, hard.*

10. Growing up, all I ever wanted was to be told that I was beautiful just like you, but I think I just wanted to be like you in any way. Now when I do my makeup I draw your mole onto my face.

Hoki Mai

She kisses him goodbye with her eyes still wet and alight from their last swim in the Awatere River. At the train station celebration, she leads the kapa haka but her voice keeps breaking under and over itself like waves. Like last night, on the riverbank, between the moss and the baby's-breath, where he had kissed her sticky until she cried out from her chest. And she was thinking about the rolls of white fabric her sister kept in the shed and how she would make a dress pressed with shiny bits of shell. She could even fix a veil from a fishing net or wear knots of pale hydrangeas like a crown upon her head. Then together they would move to the empty plot of ancestral land forgotten by the sea and have little brown babies that she would make sure to stuff fat with potatoes and wobbly mutton. And her children would slurp kina in the summer. Collect driftwood for the fires on their way home from school. And their father would take up a good job in Gisborne. Return home, with sacks of boiled sweets and powdery jam-filled treats, and maybe, on special occasions, a European perfume or powder that she would keep but never use. And already she could smell the florals and the meat. Feel them turning inside her. Sensations so visceral that she cried out from her chest but when the sun lit up and the train started pulling away, with every salute, march and funeral-wave farewell, she felt the world changing. The lump in her throat swelled like a sea that threatened to take him from her, and she had to swallow hard. But she promised that every day she would be the first to check the mail and that was the only vow she took.

Nobody in the Water

Nobody goes near the lake anymore, not since
they found that swollen brown body floating
amongst the pōhutukawa leaves and beer cans.
Nobody goes near the lake anymore, because
it smells acrid and sour. The surface has curdled
chewy like spoilt milk, or so we imagine, because
nobody goes near the lake anymore and nobody
feeds the ducks Budget white bread. Instead they eat
discarded fish and chips outside the shops and die
in the mouths of red-collared pit bulls. So even
the ducks don't go near the lake anymore because
nobody goes near the lake anymore, but people drive past
and remember to lock their doors and warn their children.
Nobody goes near the lake anymore because it stains
like shame in the thick skin of the city and really
nobody goes near the lake anymore because nobody
ever did. And one could guess, that's probably why
his body ended up in there, floating in the first place.

Christmas

We drink your grandad's vodka
from 1955.

It goes down smooth and terrible
and suddenly we are alight

and dancing with phantom photocopies
of our fathers.

I wish we could have watched them
fall in love

with our mothers.
All we have ever known

is the feeling of somebody leaving.
Dr Martens sound like gunshots

down rimu hallways and the taste
of copper on somebody's tongue isn't love.

But sometimes it's easier to pretend it is.
And it's easier to ignore the engines

outside our bedroom windows
filling the glass with fog. In the morning

the PlayStation is gone but
not the tyre marks in the gravel.

Long White Clouds

all anyone ever does around here is / grow weed and stare / into
burnt-out houses / into the rabbit hole / into the cards / into the skin /
and roll their cars / their eyes / their r's / their cigarettes / and kick
snow / kick rugby balls / kick each other / kick bad habits / only to
find another / like an eel / in the creek / in the backyard / in the dark /
in winter / and try to kill it on the rocks / chase the girls / in a shed / a
bathtub / a bed / with wet fingers / eyes / tongues / and T-shirts / from
spilled beer / spilled cum / spilled blood / spilled secrets / bad boys /
with bad skin / bad tattoos / and bad reputations / because here / all
anyone ever does is / swear / across their hearts / at referees / at other
drivers / taking to the road / cos all anyone ever wants around here
is / out / of home / of the closet / of the relationship / of the sixth-
storey window / open it / to the cold / to the clouds / to the sky / cos
all anyone ever does around here is / dive /

LBD

there is a dark-skinned darkness in me / I wear her like a little black dress / Gucci / velvet-pressed / embroidered roses on thin blue eyelids / a fault in my blood like I'm violent / moving in the club like I'm walking on water / no miracle though / mouth red like a fire engine / hair falling like debris / I grew up / on the sound of women wailing / now they wail for me / I carry them inside me / bones vibrating like a ringtone / red phone dialling / he is nervous and I'm lying / listen to me hiding / in the matte-black bathroom / call a cab for me soon / I want to drown / in a bathtub / carved out / of rose gold / fill it up with champagne and / shame too thick to choke down / I want to dissolve / into night / it fits / tight and acidic / like a womb / the Parisian catacombs / tombs / of bland white skulls / other lovers on display / mounted on the walls / of his apartment / on the bed of / my tongue / I am the dress you wear / to your funeral / I am the dress you wear / then it comes off

Watching the Boys Play Rugby

like flies swarming
in black tidal pools or

a milky way of sluts in short
shorts and long socks, Catholic

schoolboys teasing each other
in the scrum. Bull-headed matadors

depending on the score. The music
of bones in their noses all smashed

and spitty like pop rock candy.
Make a pit-stop at the dairy,

buy a scoop of chips to throw
at the seagulls who can't be scared off,

red-eyed demons watching
the boys play rugby. Eat too much or

not enough. Throats dry but mouths
open and over-glossed

when the game is over, and the boys
come orbiting the car

with pale moon faces, either
luminous or crumbling.

Pania

When she worked in Auckland her name was Cheetah but when she worked in Sydney she called herself Pania. When the men who paid asked her *What do you want to do with your life* she told them she was desperate to return to the ocean, and that's why, once summer was over and she had saved enough money, she was going back to school to study marine biology. It's not an original story. But one day a man quieter than the usual kind told her that when he was nine he'd had a goldfish who died and his mother told him to flush it down the toilet, only he couldn't because he loved it, and with every soft, half-hearted flush the fish would be resurrected, swimming for a few seconds in the bottom of the bowl. She told him that once she won a goldfish in a river-dancing contest and she had to carry it home in a little plastic bubble. The sky parted like split skin and in the rain she slipped and smashed into the hard edge where the kerb met the gutter. Her heart popped as she watched her little prized fish roll and slip away like a girl with a free drink, down a stormwater drain. *Unbelievable*, he exclaimed. *Exactly*, she agreed.

2

He ran his tongue over her bruised knees and she was immediately
overwhelmed by the intimacy between skin and bone, by the feeling
of his wet front teeth, by the wetness of her purple and yellow
trauma swelling just beneath the surface. It was always there,
an invisible pollution, but finally it had risen and—dear God—
somebody wanted to kiss it. Sometimes her body was a swimming
pool full of dead bees and foliage, and sometimes she liked that
better. It kept the delicate boys away. When she was little and lived
by the sea, she swam a lot and was fearless with her body. She let
herself be thrashed and turned about by wave after wave, this way
and that way. Her grandmother always said *Never turn your back on
the ocean*, because you never knew what might be coming in. She
used to think about sharks and stingrays, then tidal waves, then she
thought about a horizon full of big white sails. Still, she always felt
safe in the water, and she welcomed the invasion.

3

After she let him roll on top of her, he wanted to go to the clinic
to get checked and she waited in the car, embarrassed, but when
he came back he told her that he wanted to tell people about her
and she said, *You can't.* He asked why and she sighed and tried to
explain that she was a creature of the ocean and if she didn't return
when it called her, she would die. He got mad after that and pushed
his thumb into the yellow tender bruise until she let out a small cry
but later that night he came to her and apologised with two tickets
to Vanuatu cos he went there once with some friends he made in
his scuba-diving class and it had changed his life. She asked if she
could exchange them for a flight to Napier where her grandmother
was busy dying. Only she wasn't. He Facebooked one of her cousins
and sent pictures to her family— ones she didn't know he had
taken. It wasn't often that she felt naked, but when she did it caused
her whole body to dry out into a dusty shudder. She tried to call her
mother, but there was no answer. She went to work and tried to put
her hurt aside for the night. He arrived and grabbed her face in the
dark blood-velvet corner and accused her of lying. *Yes,* she hissed
through bubbling lips, *I never won a stupid goldfish.*

Baptism

Wearing a La Perla G-string
that costs more than your weekly rent
you feel yourself reborn with every
dripping plastic dollar. You pray
that it comes in waves. A tsunami
that will sweep your skin
from your pearlescent bones
and transform you into a myth,
into a jade-tailed mermaid.
In a fish-tank filled with pink light
you wash the touches out of your hair.
The men stare with eyelids
heavy from alcohol, the same
half-shut way that God probably regards us all.

Takeaways

years old / French-kissed like
soft serve / hands pinned up /
against the wall / school picture /
slipping off / the refrigerator / party
thumping through / the walls too tall
to slip away from / too small to not be /
swallowed / like a pale blue pill / a
chill snaps & throws ice / across her
stomach / sister watches her vomit
in her play-kitchen kettle / but she doesn't tell /
when the party crumbles / & gives way to
something else / they play their own games /
two sisters in the closet / playing who can keep /
quiet the longest? last until / they have to get in
the car / boyfriend's got a baseball bat and their
mother's heart / beating / flying / 160 k's across
the motorway / in flammable pink pyjamas / next
town over / mother stops the car / let's go / get
something to eat / not sure if she can / stomach
anything anymore / but the only time they ever got
happy meals / was when it was the hardest to be / _.

Shame

helen clark announced
that she wet herself
listening to annie crummer
singing at a concert fundraiser

to resurrect hinerupe marae
which burned to the ground
in an accidental and
non-government-related fire

it was raining and the plastic seats
were from the seventies
and round

she stood up
and everybody applauded her
for being a good sport

you know this story because
your grandmother wrote it down
in a brown photo album
she kept poorly hidden

there was a torn photograph
of a soldier and on the back
it was written that once
your grandmother was in love
with two brothers

lost one to the sea and in her grief
opened her jaw
like a whale and
hooked up with the other

but they couldn't stay together
because of the children

or maybe that was the story of papatūānuku

all those maari stories
are the same
your uncle says with
a pained expression

you notice that he tends to talk
loudly when he doesn't want to listen

when he was little
he went to school
and often got in trouble
for talking—

a lot of shit

which would never get him anywhere

and only ever got him hit

the winz lady who smiles
has a sign in her office that says
he aha te mea nui o te ao
he tangata, he tangata, he tangata

but she says the most important thing
in the world
is getting back into the workforce

she is proud of her job and
maintains a tiny appearance

she has a slick vaselined bun
and pats your head as you leave

back out through the waiting room
where everyone keeps
their eyes on the ground

in primary school
the kapa haka tutor is usually
16 and pretty
can sing really well but
her taniwha mouth
splits open when she yells

eyes up ladies! smile girls!
be proud!

once you saw her making out
at a park against
a multicoloured rock-climbing wall

her school skirt was gathered at
her hipbones and
her legs were off the ground

she wasn't even embarrassed
the next day she came to school
with a bruise that looked like
someone had taken a bite
out of an overripe plum

you watched whaea's eyes
swell wider than the pacific ocean
as she dragged her outside
by the root of her extensions

and she still wasn't even embarrassed

one day when you are 16 and shy
he asks if you can stay behind
your mum is waiting in the car park but
you don't want to say so
so you say um sure yes I guess so

and he says he wants you
to read him your work which makes you
take a step back from the desk like
a wind-up doll

your voice is small
when you say you can't and he says you can

you say it's bad
he says he highly doubts that and you

betray yourself with a smile that
slips from you like your school bag
makes a dull thump on the floor

he stands up while you read and you can see him
moving in your peripherals
you stutter and try to concentrate on the lines
in your 1B5 but they're a blur

you hope he doesn't notice
but he tells you to keep your chin up
with his fingers

then he asks
why are you so nervous?

3

Vampires versus Werewolves

What was it like to grow up during the Twilight *season?*

> My high school was surrounded by pine trees
> and a dank fog from a student body
> of chain smokers. It was romantic.

Could you be more specific?

> In science, we didn't study mitosis
> but the purple swimming pools on each other's necks.
> They sprouted spotty like hydrangeas
> out of navy V-neck sweaters.
> I grew up worrying that strangers could read my mind.

Could you be more specific?

> I couldn't keep my thoughts clean or my head in.
> No one could.
> We were two sides of the same hood.

Could you be more specific?

> Red & Blue. White & Black.

Could you be more specific?

> We had brown boys running around topless during PE
> and calling themselves the wolf pack and the white girls
> took them home to see if their parents would bare their teeth.

Could you be more specific?

So the boys were served up like hunks of raw meat.
But at least they got to eat out at fancy restaurants and in bedrooms
covered in posters from *Creme* and *Dolly* magazines.

Could you be more specific?

I had Edward Cullen on my wall.

Could you be more specific?

Taylor Lautner dated Taylor Swift.
Robert Pattinson dated FKA Twigs.

Could you be more specific?

I guess I see myself in her in the same way I see myself
in the twigs on the ground. Organic, snapped, brown.

Could you be more specific?

Brown reminds me of the leaves and
sausage roll wrappers in the gutters.

Could you be more specific?

We used to say 'guttered' when something bad
or funny-sad happened.
You left your phone on the bus? Guttered.
The teacher kept you in? Guttered.
You can't come to the party cos you have to

babysit your siblings while your mum
is at housie? Guttered.
I think we were trying to say *gutted*
as if we felt as though our stomachs
had been knifed and emptied out.

Could you be more specific?

It's easy to be seen as the big bad wolf.
Fourteen, chronically shy, anorexic.
You make yourself sick with lusting.
All you want is that pale sparkling on the television.
It makes you do things out of character
or, it would if you had a character.
That's why fingers end up down throats and up skirts
and pointing in the wrong direction.

Could you be more specific?

It's the boy who cried wolf,
but in reverse you cry sheep and
nobody believes your bleating.

Could you be more specific?

They don't want to.

Could you be more specific?

I don't want to.

Could you be more specific?

I remember once after swimming
a girl was sobbing
because she was teased
about the thick dark hair
growing like a forest
across her arms and stomach.
Now everyone
draws on their eyebrows
just like hers.

Could you be more specific?

It was Sports Day
but after that
the administration banned the girls
from wearing crop-tops and bikinis
but the boys
still ran around in Y-fronts
and purple acrylic paint.

Could you be more specific?

The boys were running from their mothers
and the girls who looked like their mothers.

Could you be more specific?

You're just not exotic
to people who look like you.

Could you be more specific?

You want what you can't have.

Could you be more specific?

Edward Cullen only wanted Bella
because he couldn't read her mind.

Could you be more specific?

That, and she smelt like wild
strawberries or some bullshit.

Could you be more specific?

He wouldn't have wanted her if
she was like those other girls
whose minds
he was always sneering at
but always reading
like a teen magazine or . . .
. . . like a trashy book.

Could you be more specific?

Well he was an angsty
stone-cold son of a bitch . . .

always flaking on her,
ignoring her,
telling her to leave him alone.

Could you be more specific?

Then just, like, showing up,
in her bedroom,
uninvited,
in the middle of the night,
watching her sleep,
spying on her,
and generally being
weird
and mean
and obsessive.
And this was all on top of
telling her constantly
how badly he wanted to
suck the life from her
already lifeless veins.

Could you be more specific?

We crave otherness.
We hate otherness.

Could you be more specific?

There was a boy who would meet
another boy in the pine trees
but after accidently making
eye contact in the hallway
he put that boy's head through a locker.

Could you be more specific?

In *Twilight*, the vampires and wolves

made a pact to live in peace as long as
they left each other alone.

Could you be more specific?

But then high school happened
and we liked the look of one another's teeth.

Scabbing

Year 9. Ex-boyfriend makes $50
scabbing schoolkids for a dollar
during a single lunchtime.
Upon hearing this news, I instantly regret
breaking up with him via my best friend's text
a few months earlier.
I broke up with him because I was 12
but also because I was in love
with somebody else and I had only agreed
to go out with him in the first place because
my best friend was dating *his best friend*
at the time and being the Libra that I am
I made the diplomatic decision to date him
to be nice . . . However!
His best friend cheated
on *my best friend* at camp with a girl
who, at age 13, was the youngest ever
bogan beauty queen of the Greater Wellington Region.
So, in a sense, who could blame him?
But after that, dating his friend became tricky—
a matter of playground custody, and I had no access
to legal advice. Didn't think twice when I gave the okay
mafia nod to my number two, who texted:

she's got no time
4 u sorry she really
wants 2 focus on her
career right now bye.

My best friend would like to point out
that he cried. I cried too as soon as I knew
that boy was a hustler, my kinda man,
a go-getter, who knew how to stack
that shiny 1-dollar gold paper.

To make matters worse
he's a proper rugby player now.

I fantasise about being his housewife.
I imagine the interviews in *Woman's Weekly*
where he says things like

I've had a crush
on this girl since
I was 12 years old.

I imagine that he takes me to dinners and balls
and all his friends' wives become
prejudiced with jealousy,
having had to work so hard
in gyms and DMs and stuntin'
on Instagram but mine
is so in love with me
that I don't even have to try
(think Zoë Kravitz meets
indigenous demigoddess)
cos I've been his ride-or-die
Bonnie-and-Clyde kinda bitch
since I was 12 years old.
On a talk show, the host pulls up
embarrassing old photos of the formal
we never went to together. He laughs

in joyous surprise while I cringe in a cute
and charming Libra kind of way—
earning me my place as an adored Kiwi socialite
(think Aja Rock meets Pocahontas).
When we go home,
to our waterfront apartment, we fuck
like we want to have a heart attack
and die together
living that death-do-us-part kind of love.

Assimilation

they consider
themselves to be
a modern couple

they take turns

giving
and receiving
oral

they split the bills
evenly and they share
the chores but

when he brings in
the washing
he leaves the pegs
all over the ground

he doesn't bother to
pick them up
and put them back
into the basket

and she considers this to be
culturally insensitive

and as progressive
as they are
she can't help

but think about
potatoes and muskets
disease-ridden blankets
surveyors and preachers

and how many Māori girls
ended up on their knees
in order to erect
this modern nation

she sighs
and rolls her eyes
like a tiny haka

as she pulls the last
remaining peg embedded
in the mud with the last
of her mana

she could either lick them clean
with the sponge of her tongue

or

plunge them back into the earth's
dark wet cunt. Let her husband pick them up.

Red American Mustang

Love u so much . . . Ur touch is soft like . . . an Elvis Presley love song to Hawai'i, his mistress . . . Too bad u serenade with a sailor's mouth . . . lucky I'm an ocean parting for your figurehead & . . . waiting to be . . . entered. Ur privilege . . . is addictive & sexy like . . . the finest . . . Cuban cocaine! And I'm a stack of ngatas . . . I'm on spring break in Miami & ur my yayo daddy I'm an alligator! & ur . . . above the law. *Shoot me quick Cupid! I'm a dangerous native!* u drive me deep into the wild. I feel . . . dislocated! in ur eyes the colour of money or . . . a forest on fire. Ur just so classically handsome! Like . . . a red American Mustang & I'm your tiny dashboard dancer . . . keeping your eyes off the road . . .

Red-blooded Males

Your father didn't speak to me
the first two times I saw him. You said
you used to go hunting together sometimes
for weeks on end, hardly speaking.
I imagine the two of you
silently camouflaged and deceiving
weepy-eyed does drinking from the foot
of a waterfall, innocent
to the sound of size 11 boots
crushing the life out of clovers. It's funny
the difference between what you notice
and what takes notice of you.

Your mother's dresser covered in pig tusks
and ram skulls housing silver rings and
a single bottle of Estée Lauder foundation
too pink for me to use but made her look
like rare meat. Seven lucky stag heads stabbed
into the walls made her feel like she was
being watched at all times. I should've helped
her cook and wash the dishes. Instead I drank
Heinekens until I was slack-jawed enough to
make fun of his music. The only metal I like
is gold and hangs around the neck of a rapper.
He positioned his thumb and trigger finger
on the dial, turned it up, and smiled. I said no—

I've never been hunting. I'm a vegetarian
but I did see a taxidermied cat in a feather headdress
pulling a tiny wooden chariot at a museum once.
After your mother left him, he came down
to visit us. We went to a bar filled with dried flowers
and left-over Halloween decorations.
I comment on the little plastic skeletons
between sips, and he says, *You strike me as a details girl*
whatever that means. But coolly I said yeah.
I try to notice things. I'm a modern city woman.
I practise mindfulness. I'm trying to reach nirvana.
When it's my turn to buy the drinks he tells his friend
to slip me a ngata, and he puts it in my bra.

When drunk and asked what I would do
if I was lost in the forest and I came across
what I thought was a fire in the distance
I said I would get scared and die
like that time I was on the Hair Raiser in Luna Park
overlooking Sydney and felt my soul leave my body
in an easy resignation. He said,
You don't strike me as the type of girl who would just give up.
I shrugged. I didn't know I had anything worth
giving up in the first place. Once Mum tried
to scare my sister and me by grabbing us
as we finished our makeup in the bathroom.
I froze and tried to slip down the wall. My sister
punched her in her nose. Not sure who learned

The only time your father ever hit you
was when you pointed your shotgun
in his direction.
The number one rule of hunting is
never aim your gun at anything
you don't intend to kill.
He brought his palm to your head
and the words still rattle around
in your skull like tinnitus.
So you didn't hear me wince when
you showed me the skin of a deer
you killed at 16, spotty like Bambi
cos you shot her in the summer.
Your father walked in eating a bowl
of mince, laughed and showed me his
kill, because his kill was bigger.

In your childhood bedroom I made you
cover the taxidermied boar on the wall
with a towel before I even thought about
taking my clothes off. You touched me
but pulled your hand away quickly
cos I was hot and slimy like a deer heart.
Your embarrassment softened you
into confession. Admitted that once
you accidently shot an expecting mother
and watched with pooling horror as your father
plunged his bare hands into the burning carcass
and pulled the baby out. You watched him
snap its neck. You thought he would

give it mouth to mouth. He wiped
his hands on your khaki T-shirt and
your mother couldn't wash it out.

wtn boys

soft wellington boys in six hundred
dollar leather want to send me their poetry
& tie me to their beds so I tell them I like their
fathers instead & listen to their aluminium skulls
crack like coke cans and thunder.

A Sugar Daddy Is Essentially an Arts Patron

R says, singling out a pair of diamante cowboy boots on Dollskill. The man he is messaging gives him a budget for his performance outfits that includes the cost of lingerie. We give each other the look (dark-eyed, catty). *You could just buy expensive Calvin Kleins and say you misunderstood?* It's the lingerie that makes R nervous, and he types *how to avoid* into Google. The simple answer is *you say no* but it's a harsh combination of consonant and vowel sounds and sometimes they just aren't musical enough for the moment. But it's best to stay suspicious. From a helicopter even the driest places like the Desert Road can look like French vanilla ice cream dusted with expensive cacao. And when the wind and wine and adrenaline steal even the taste of words from your mouth, be thankful he has the resources to replace them. Generosity is an intoxicating pretty weed. Like mistletoe. And in the season of giving, sometimes you just feel like gifting yourself to someone special. Sometimes you want to wrap yourself up in a red dress and fox fur, tie a ribbon in your hair and make Christmas come early. But most of the time Christmas sucks and you end up feeling like you're babysitting a kid who wants to show someone all of their cool things. You rehearse your gasp which should sound as genuine as an orgasm. *I've never seen anything like this before!* Even though you've seen a harbour before. Even though you've seen a Kubrick film before. You've definitely seen a car before. So to cause trouble you say you love 'Can You Feel the Love Tonight?' by the Beatles. R says, *Ugh, he likes the Beatles.* R won't tolerate long nights of chalky musical education. He waits for him to buy the shoes, then he blocks him. *If you want to walk the line,* he says wisely, winking and blowing on his fingers, you *have to know where to draw it.* Then he puts his gun away.

Black Velvet Mini

I

She plays Hendrix on
guitar at her teen daughter's party.
She finds a room full of Gregg Araki
cyberspace stoners who recommend
a remedy for her shoulders
the bones softened and sore from the weight
of religious condemnation.
So she gives up the Bible verses.
Takes her Chanel chains off.
Grows wings. Levitates. With a light touch
plucks out 'All Along the Watchtower'
as deftly as she can pluck
feathers off a chicken.
And fuck. And feed a family.
Manage a farm. Still manages to run
every morning and evening past
paddocks of cows and Chryslers, past
dirty farmers and their dirty sons
until she is pencil thin. Draws attention
to herself. Inspires comments from strangers.
Like a muse. Used. Crumpled like
a chippie packet. She eats the entire bag
and laughs. Forgets her sentences. Remembers
how it feels to have her body strummed
by wind coming in from the ocean. The way
the taste of wild mint is like an echo
in her mouth. How hunger feels like hellfires
and hope feels like walking up a dead riverbed
searching for a trickle.